The family of Abraham

English text: Liam Kelly - Anne White
Original text: Albert Hari - Charles Singer

Illustrations: Mariano Valsesia - Betti Ferrero

CHAPTER • 1

Abraham sets out

Marc Chagall
(1887-1985),
Abraham and the Three
Angels

There is something dream-like about this painting. The edges are blurry and the main figures look familiar, but not quite. It represents a mysterious event in Abraham's life. He welcomed three visitors, gave them food and drink and a place to rest. In return they promised that Abraham and Sara would have a son.

Leaving

A nomad in the Libyan desert

Near the town of Ur (in the country now called Iraq) a tribe of wandering shepherds breaks camp. They pull up the tent pegs. They fold up the big black canvas. They pack their belongings onto their donkeys. The caravan sets off, leaving Ur behind with all its temples and gods.

Why did Terah and his son Abram (or Abraham) pack up and leave ? They were not the only ones. Around 1850 BC life became difficult for the wandering shepherds (nomads). They were looked down on by the new town rulers. They were constantly harassed by the city officials. They began to dream of a peaceful countryside, and rich grazing land far away from towns and cities. So off they set on a long and winding journey.

The first big stopping-place was near Haran (south of modern-day Turkey, near the Syrian border). From there, after a little while, Abraham set off leaving his native land for good.

A donkey carrying food in Greece

Abraham's faith

The story of Abraham's journey was passed down by word of mouth, from parent to child. When, after several centuries*, the writers of the Bible wrote down the details of this journey, they insisted on making several important points:

1. Abraham's journey isn't just the start of a migration of peoples. It's a response to God's call.
2. Abraham is presented as the first great believer. He leaves his country and his pagan idols to follow the one God.
3. Abraham's call is like a seed. From it grows the whole history of humankind. All the nations of the earth are blessed in Abraham.

***After several centuries**
Abraham lived about 1850 BC. The parts of the Bible which tell his story were written between 1000 BC and 500 BC. They tell us how the Bible people understood their ancestor's life and his faith.

B i b l e

God said

Genesis, chapter 12, verses 1 to 7.

The LORD said to Abram, *"Leave your country, your relatives, and your father's home, and go to a land that I am going to show you. I will give you many descendants, and they will become a great nation. I will bless you and make your name famous, so that you will be a blessing.*

I will bless those who bless you, But I will curse those who curse you. And through you I will bless all the nations."

When Abram was 75 years old, he started out from Haran, as the Lord had told him to do; and Lot went with him.

Abram took his wife Sarai, his nephew Lot, and all the wealth and all the slaves they had acquired in Haran, and they started out for the land of Canaan.

When they arrived in Canaan, Abram travelled through the land until he came to the sacred tree of Moreh, the holy place of Shechem. (At that time the Canaanites were still living in the land.) The LORD appeared to Abram and said to him, *"This is the country that I am going to give to your descendants."*

Abram and Abraham

Notice how God changes Abraham's name. Abram (which means *"great because of his father"*) is going to become Abraham (which means *"father of a great people"*). In the Bible, changing your name means changing your direction in life.

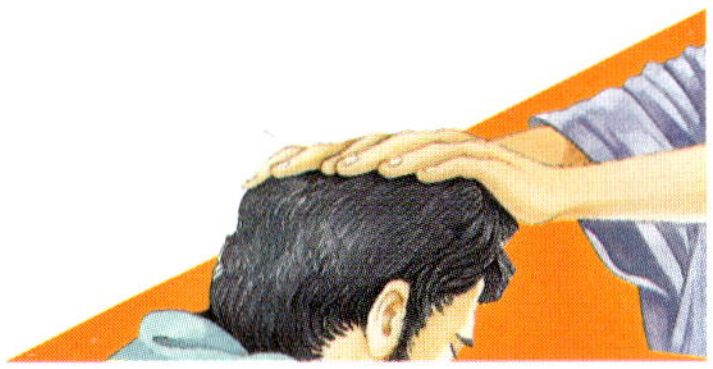

Blessing

God blesses Abraham. That means God wants to make him happy - Abraham himself, his family and all human beings. In the Bible joy, peace, friendship and prosperity are thought of as gifts (blessings) from God.

Canaan

This is the country where Jesus will live.
It will be called Palestine.
Today it is made up of Israel and the Palestinian self-governing regions.

Today

God is near

God speaks

God invites human beings to friendship. God doesn't stay far off! Like a loving father he cares passionately about his children. It is quite natural that God should speak like a person, like a father or mother to the child they love.

Conscience

This "dialogue" with God is what people who believe in God mean by 'conscience' - (con = with; science from 'to know'). It is a way of saying that deep in our hearts we can be in conversation with God. This helps us 'to hear' God's word in our lives.

God calls

Deep in their hearts, God calls to human beings. It's a call to set out and become children of God, fully human people. It is a call to love God and our neighbours.

Leaving

Hearing God's call and choosing to be faithful to God is like setting out on a long journey! It means going forward, despite difficulties, on a journey through life. Then day by day we will become true children of God and brothers and sisters to our neighbours.

Blessing

God blesses every child, God blesses the whole human race. What God wants is for everyone to do well, and to be happy. God's plan is a happiness that will last forever. God speaks in Jesus. He is the Son of God who makes known God's loving plan for all creation.

Setting out

It is hard to set out
and scary too
even when you feel sure
God is calling to you.
'Will I know the roads ?
If I lose my nerve,
or don't like where they lead,
will God still be there ?'

'Will I have to change
the way I live
think of others first
learn to share and give ?'

Setting out is okay
if trust can grow.
If you come to believe
that wherever you go
God is near,
God is close,
God's the best of guides,
a companion who will
always be at your side.

CHAPTER 2

A long journey

Horace Vernet, (1789-1863),
Agar is banished by Abraham

Look at the faces of the three people. What do you think they are saying, thinking and feeling ?

© Giraudon - Musée des Beaux-Arts, Nantes (France)

A great traveller

Children on a donkey in Judea

In Abraham's time, farmers whose herds were small beasts, like sheep and goats, had to move from place to place quite often to find better grazing land. (This made them 'nomads', travellers.) They drove their animals around the Fertile Crescent, at the edge of the desert, wherever they could find watering places for their flocks.

Abraham was a great traveller. He crossed the Fertile Crescent: from Ur (in Mesopotamia), through Haran (in Syria), Canaan, the Negeb Desert, through Egypt, and then back again to settle in Canaan. Throughout his journey, like all nomads, he had two dreams: that he would have lots of children, and that one day he would own a stretch of land.*

A double promise

The Bible does not talk about what Abraham hoped for, but about God's promise: Abraham would have many descendants and would have land to call his own. It takes a long time for these promises to come true. Abraham left his own country. He arrived in Canaan. God promised him the land, but what a disappointment: the land is hit by drought! Abraham went to Egypt. His wife was captured by the Pharoah. He got her back and returned to Canaan. He set up his nephew Lot to get things going in the greenest part of the land, the Jordan valley. Meanwhile, Abraham travelled to the dry mountain region. God had also promised him children, but Abraham's wife is barren. According to the customs of those days he decided to try and have a child by his servant Hagar. He is named *"Ishmael"*** Will Ishmael inherit the promises of God ? God's promise is to Sarah. Even though she was old, she had a son, *"Isaac"*. Then everything was called into question. God asked Abraham to sacrifice his son. Abraham agreed. But Isaac lives. He has a family. Only at the end of his life does Abraham get the first 'parcel' of the Promised Land. He buys a field in which to bury his wife. By telling the story of Abraham in this way, the author wanted to show that the way of faith is often very difficult

A Dromedary camel in the Egyptian desert

** Throughout his long journey, Abraham and his tribe travelled through the following modern places: Iraq, Syria, Lebanon, Israel, Palestine and Egypt.*
See the map on page 35.

*** See page 11 :* **Ishmael**

Count the stars

Genesis, chapter 12, verse 10; chapter 13, verses 1, 12.14-15; chapter 17, verese 4-5; chapter 21, verses 2, 3 and 6

There was a famine in Canaan, and it was so bad that Abram went farther south to Egypt, to live there for a while... Abram went north out of Egypt to the southern part of Canaan with his wife and everything he owned, and Lot went with him... Abram stayed in the land of Canaan, and Lot settled among the cities in the valley and camped near Sodom...

After Lot had left, the LORD said to Abram, *"From where you are look carefully in all directions. I am going to give you and your descendants all the land that you see, and it will be yours for ever..."*

"Look at the sky and try to count the stars; you will have as many descendants as that."

"I make this covenant with you; I promise that you will be the ancestor of many nations. Your name will no longer be Abram but Abraham..."

The LORD blessed Sarah...and she became pregnant and bore a son to Abraham when he was old. Abraham named him Isaac... Sarah said, *"God has brought me joy and laughter. Everyone who hears about it will laugh with me."*

Ishmael

The son of Abraham and his servant Hagar. His name means: *"God has listened"*. He is considered as the ancestor of the Arabs.

Descendants

Abraham's descendants are not just those who were born into his family. His children will be as many as the stars in the sky, as many as the whole human race.

Isaac

The son of Abraham and his wife Sarah. To show how important this birth is to be, the author tells Sarah's story in great detail. Her age is no barrier. Isaac's name means "God will laugh". Because he was born to such an old mother, everybody did laugh and he brought joy to his parents. He becomes the father of Jacob, the ancestor of the tribes of Israel.

Today

A family too many to count

A personal appeal

God calls Abraham by his name, just as parents name their precious new baby. Through Abraham, all who are his children in faith hear the call of God as the voice of a loving parent calling them by name.

Promise

Through Abraham, a promise is made by God to all the children of the earth. I will love you always. I will keep watch over you. I will never abandon you, nothing can ever break this promise. God's word lasts forever.

Trust

Trusting God means believing in God. It means being sure that God only wants the best for each person on earth.

Doubt

Life is tough. Sometimes faith is tested. You can sometimes feel that you are all alone and that God is not bothered with you anymore. It's at times like that you need to think again about God's promise. God is faithful, even though God's way may seem mysterious.

On the move

Someone who believes is a bit like a nomad. Nomads are always on the move, always changing places, always on the road. God's call keeps believers moving forward, travelling steadily from one place to the next, trying each day to live as people 'created in God's image'.

With God

With God
we're always setting out:
no time to get bored
or to get stuck in routine.

With God
were always on the move:
no time to get stuck
in our own little world.

With God
there's always a wind at play
bringing joy to your heart,
and urging you on.

With God
there's always bread to share
food for the journey
to keep you strong.

With God
there's always a hand to help
to lift you up
and to pull you on.

With God
you will come to an open door
with everyone cheering
because you're home.

Happiness is with God.

CHAPTER • 3

Isaac, the longed-for son

Jacques le Grant
The sacrifice of Abraham,
a 15th century miniature

The vivid colours call attention to the importance of the scene. What story is the picture telling ? Share your ideas with a friend.

Human sacrifices

Maize harvest in Romania

In Abraham's day some people practised human sacrifice. They thought that by doing this they would please their gods and get them on their side. Then there would be good harvests and protection from their enemies. Abraham certainly knew about these practices. Perhaps even he - newly arrived in the country - wondered if he should imitate the Canaanites. Perhaps he would please his God by offering his son as a human sacrifice. But of course he did not.

A Hittite character presenting a sheaf of wheat as an offering. Carving from Ivriz in Turkey

God does not want this

About 1000 years later, a writer put together one of the most beautiful texts of the Old Testament: the sacrifice, or the binding, of Isaac. "Binding" (tying) means that he was tied up on the altar, but not sacrificed.

The author writes this story as if it were a test for Abraham. How far would his faith go ? But the writer particularly wants to show that God refuses to accept human sacrifices. It took time for the practice to die out. Even in Israel, some kings were tempted to sacrifice their sons to get favours from their god.* What happened with Abraham makes it clear: God wants none of it.**

Statue of Gustav Vigeland in Oslo, Norway

** According to the Bible, in the 8th century BC, the king of Judah, Ahaz, "gave his son over to the fire" (II Kings 16:3). This means he offered his son in sacrifice probably to a foreign god. He thought this would bring him the god's protection against the enemies who were threatening Jerusalem.*

*** The Bible strongly condemns child sacrifices offered to a god called "Molech".*

Bible

The sacrifice of Isaac

Genesis, chapter 22, verses 1 to 17.

Some time later God tested Abraham; he called to him, *"Abraham!"* And Abraham answered, *"Yes, here I am!" "Take your son,"* God said, *"your only son Isaac, whom you love so much, and go to the land of Moriah. There on a mountain that I will show you, offer him as a sacrifice to me."*

Early the next morning Abraham cut some wood for the sacrifice, loaded his donkey, and took Isaac and two servants with him. They started out for the place that God had told him about. On the third day Abraham saw the place in the distance.

Abraham made Isaac carry the wood for the sacrifice, and he himself carried a knife and live coals for starting the fire. As they walked along together, Isaac said, *"Father !"* He answered, *"Yes, my son ?"* Isaac asked, *"I see that you have the coals and the wood, but where is the lamb for the sacrifice ?"* Abraham answered, *"God himself will provide one."* And the two of them walked on together.

When they came to the place which God had told him about, Abraham built an altar and arranged the wood on it. He tied up his son and placed him on the altar, on top of the wood. Then he picked up the knife to kill him. But the angel of the LORD called to him from heaven, *"Abraham, Abraham!"* He answered, *"Yes, here I am."*

"Don't hurt the boy or do anything to him," he said. *"Now I know that you honour and obey God, because you have not kept back your only son from him."* Abraham looked around and saw a ram caught in a bush by its horns. He went and got it and offered it as a burnt offering instead of his son...The angel of the Lord called to Abraham from heaven a second time. *"Because you did not keep back your only son from me, I promise that I will give you as many descendants as there are stars in the sky or grains of sand along the seashore."*

Your son

The author of the story wants to show how Abraham treats his son Isaac. That's why the word "son" is repeated so often. Look carefully. How does this affect the story.

Moriah

No one knows where the land of Moriah was. But later the hill on which the Temple at Jerusalem will be built is called "Mount Moriah" (II Chronicles 3:1).

Holocaust

This was a sacrifice where the whole victim (normally an animal) was completely burned. People thought that the smoke which went up into the sky carried the offering to God. The word comes from a Hebrew word "'alah" which means "to go up".

Today

God is for life

False ideas

Some people say that to please God you must suffer, injure yourself or even die! How foolish! Those are unhealthy ideas. How dare people make out that the God who made all things out of love is no better than an idol thirsting for blood !

God of love

God does not call all things into being to crush them and put impossible demands on them. God calls everyone to the fullness of his love. God is not looking for some incredible sacrifice. God is just waiting to be loved.

God of goodness

God is "*goodness*" itself. All that God does shows this. It is unbelievable that God would wish evil upon people. It is unbelievable that God would demand things which make people suffer.

Sacrifice

If you love, you don't think about "*sacrifice*" you think only of 'giving'. When you love, you prove it by offering whatever is biggest, most beautiful, and most precious. And 'biggest' and 'most beautiful' are not things. What is most precious is love in your heart, a love which thinks about the joy, honour and happiness of the one you love.

God of life

Wherever there's life, there's God. God is the source of life. God never wants people to prove their faith by dying or killing themselves. God is the "living one". God gives the breath of life to everyone to make them happy.

Searching

Since the dawn of time
the search has been on.
All over the world
are the seekers who long
to see God's face
and find God at home
unseen but near, wherever they go.

God is near at hand,
behind and beyond.
God's signs will be there
to encourage them on,
to start again
and help those who stray
so that no one is lost along the way.

All along the road
seekers meet true guides.
They proclaim God's truth
and the really good news,
that more than gold
or sacrifice rare
God prefers hearts ready to love and
care.

God's best gift of all
is Jesus, the Son.
To seekers he brings
joy and heart for the search,
they hear God's voice,
God's face becomes clear:
he is God-with-Us,
God very near.

CHAPTER • 4

Jacob the wrestler

Jacopo da Ponte
(about 1510-1592)

The artist has captured the moment when Esau gives away his birthright to his brother Jacob. Notice how the light catches their faces. What do their expressions tell you about the story ?

Life was hard

A group of camels with their owner in Judea

Life wasn't always easy for the nomads. The sun was scorching, water hard to find, and grazing land patchy. There were arguments between people and between tribes.

Abraham's descendants, living in Canaan, had kept in touch with their family who stayed in Haran, in fertile Mesopotamia.

A colourful story

The person who wrote the story of Jacob, son of Isaac, presents it as if it were a series of struggles:
Isaac had twin sons: Esau, *"the hairy one"*, who was the first-born, and Jacob, *"the heel"*. Isaac liked Esau better. Jacob was spoilt by his mother, Rebecca. The Bible tells in a colourful way how Jacob "puts his heel" on Esau. He bought Esau's rights as the first-born in exchange for a bowl of bean soup. With his mother helping him, he tricked his old blind father into giving him the blessing which should have gone to Esau. Threatened by his brother, he ran off to his uncle Laban in Haran. He quarrelled with him about marrying his daughter Rachel. After more than 14 years, he got fed up with the way he was being treated. He travelled back to Canaan afraid of a show-down with his brother Esau. He had to struggle across the River Jabbok with his family and his belongings.

The Bible story (page 22) explains to us how "the heel" became Israel*, in other words "the one who wrestled with men and with God".

** **"Israel"** is not just the new name for Jacob. His twelve sons are considered to be the fathers of the twelve tribes of Israel. The People of God in the Bible are called the "children of Israel". Their life is often a struggle. In the mysterious experiences of their ancestor Jacob, they saw themselves and their struggles. This helped them to discover God in the daily struggles of life.*

A young farming woman in Syria

Bible

Jacob wrestles with God

Genesis, chapter 32, verses 23 to 31.

That same night Jacob got up, took his two wives, his two concubines, and his eleven children, and crossed the River Jabbok. After he had sent them across, he also sent across all that he owned, but he stayed behind, alone.

Then a man came and wrestled with him until just before daybreak. When the man saw that he was not winning the struggle he struck Jacob on the hip, and it was thrown out of joint. The man said, *"Let me go; daylight is coming." "I won't unless you bless me,"* Jacob answered.

"What is your name?" the man asked. *"Jacob,"* he answered.

The man said, *"Your name will no longer be Jacob. You have struggled with God and with men, and you have won; so your name will be Israel."*

Jacob said, *"Now tell me your name."* But he answered, *"Why do you want to know my name ?"* Then he blessed Jacob.

Jacob said, *"I have seen God face to face, and I am still alive.";* so he named the place Peniel (the Face of God).

Eleven children

Jacob's twelfth child, Benjamin, was not born at this point of the story.

Alone

The Bible speaks about two lonely experiences that Jacob had. The first is when he sets out for Haran (Genesis 32: 10-22), and the second when he comes back from Haran (see text on opposite page). In the first one he discovers that the place where he was sleeping is a holy place, and in the second he discovers that getting to know God a challenge.

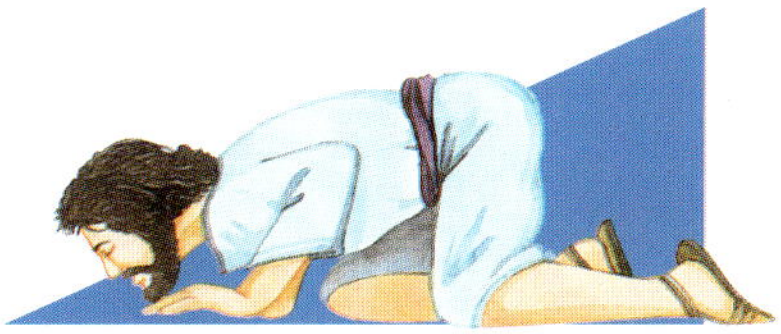

Still alive !

In those days people thought that you couldn't see God and still live.

Today

Lessons for life

Alone

Everyone has to decide for themselves, in their own heart and helped by their conscience, which roads to take in life. No one can do this for us. People can help us and give advice, but everyone has to step out themselves along the road of love, faith and courage.

A struggle

Living as a human being and a child of God is a daily challenge. It's about resisting evil which can seem easy and inviting. It's about choosing the good that can seem more difficult.

Finding my place

Everyone has to work hard to find their own place: in their family, among their friends, in the world. To be listened to, you sometimes have to shout loud or even yell! To be loved, you have to go out and get to know people. To take part in things, you have to join in with others and use your own skills to help them.

Honesty

If people are afraid of being rejected or unloved, they sometimes make up things so that others will like them. They may try to push themselves forward, shoving others aside and taking their place. They may think nothing of lying. In fact it is only themselves they fool.

Ladder

Life is often like a ladder, really high and wobbly. You need to climb carefully. Those who dare to scramble up despite their fear of heights and ignoring the splinters, get to enjoy the brilliant light at the top.

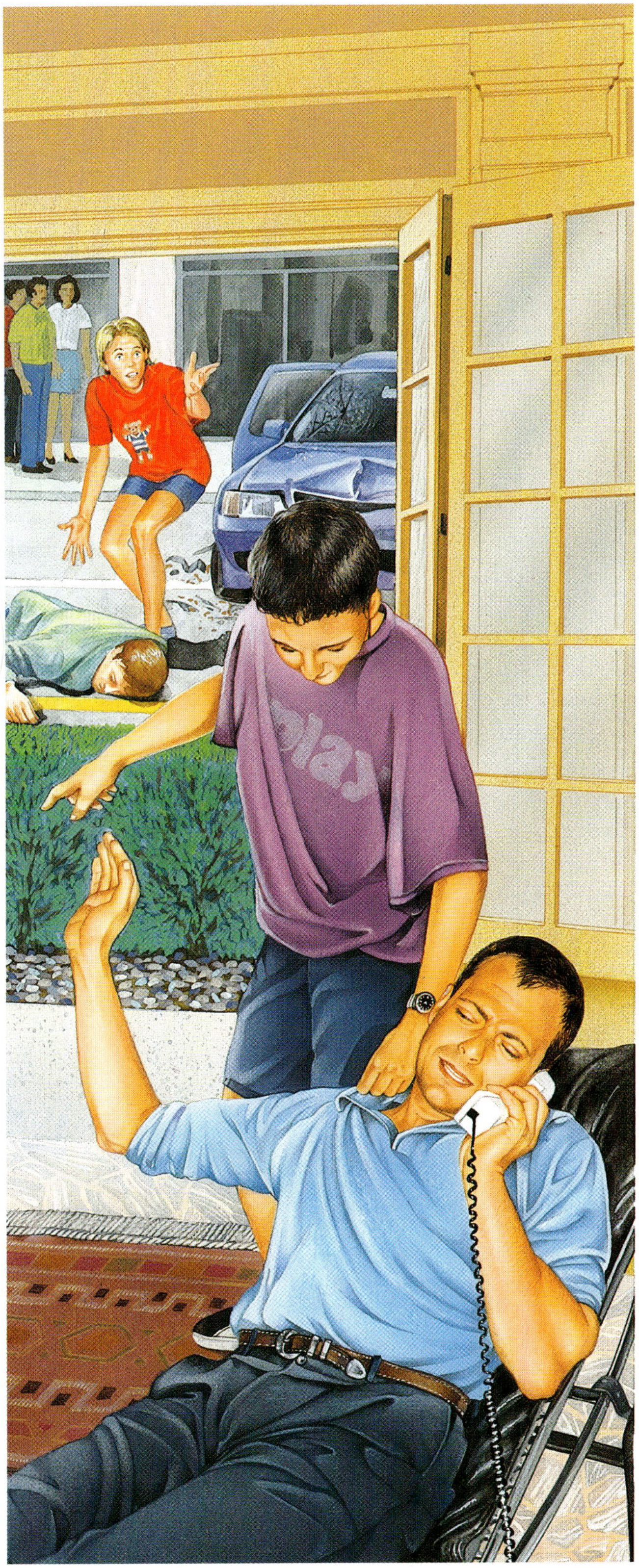

What a struggle

Life with God
brings daily challenges.

We're so cosy:
lazing around
working on half power.
God's coming
shakes us out of our drowsiness,
reminding us of the gifts we all have.
These gifts and skills
God has planted in us
are like seeds awaiting the harvest !

We're so cosy:
in our little lies which hide the fact
that we don't want to love.
God's coming reminds us
about love which never counts the cost !

We're so cosy:
nursing our grievances
and spitefulness and jealousy.
God's coming urges us to forgive
and to pray for our enemies!

What a struggle we have with God !
God is not for letting us rest.
God challenges us every day
to become even greater,
more honest,
more human:
true children of God,
and truly loved.

CHAPTER • 5

The saga of Joseph

Diego Velazquez Rodrigez de Silva (1599-1660) , Joseph's Coat is brought to Jacob.

Jealousy brought trouble between Joseph and his brothers. This is the moment when the brothers tell Jacob his favourite son is 'dead'. How do you think Jacob feels ? Are there any clues in the painting about the brothers' feelings ?

In Egypt

Nomads living in a tent in Jordan

Abraham's descendants were nomads. They travelled widely. They made contacts in Egypt. In the 17th century BC some "Shepherd Kings" (called the Hyksos*) seized control of Egypt. It became quite easy for the children of Israel to settle in Egypt and even to get important jobs. The story of Joseph reminds us of this.

A pyramid at Giza in Egypt

A really good story

The author presents Joseph as a wise** and intelligent man who gives a good example. He turns to God be his guide in the daily difficulties of life. In the story of Joseph, unlike that of Abraham, Isaac and Jacob, we never hear of God getting involved in an extraordinary way.*** The writer wants to show that God guides us in daily life, just as he guided Joseph. These pages (Genesis 37 to 50) make a really good story.

A Palestinian encampment in Judea

* **The Hyksos** *came from Asia. They introduced the horse and the war-chariot into Egypt. They were expelled around 1550 BC.*

*** The Bible contains several books of wisdom. Joseph is the perfect portrait of a "Wise" person. He puts up patiently with his lot in life. He knows when to speak and when to be silent. He becomes adviser to the King, but doesn't let it go to his head.*

**** In the story of Joseph there are no visions, mysterious voices or appearances of God or the Angel of the Lord.*

Joseph sold by his brothers

Genesis, chapter 50, verses 18 to 20.

This is the outline of the story of Joseph.
Jacob has 12 children. Joseph, Rachel's son, is his father's favourite. His brothers are jealous. They decide to sell him to travellers who are on their way to Egypt. They dip his coat in goat's blood and take it to their father to make him think that his son has been killed by a wild beast.
In Egypt, Joseph is bought by Potiphar, captain of the palace guard, and he ends up in charge of his house. But Potiphar's wife asks Joseph to go to bed with her, and he refuses. Unjustly accused, Joseph is imprisoned with two of Pharoah's servants, the master baker and the chief wine steward. They each have a dream. Joseph interprets the meaning: the wine steward will be freed and the baker will be executed. One day, Pharoah has a dream that no one can explain. Then the wine steward remembers about Joseph. Pharoah has him taken out of prison and Joseph tells him about his double dream: seven fat cows, then seven thin cows; seven ripe ears of corn and seven meagre ones. Joseph explains: *"There will be seven years with plenty of food, then seven years of famine. From now on you need to prepare for this."* Pharoah appoints Joseph governor of Egypt. During the years of plenty Joseph makes sure that the wheat is stock-piled. During the lean years he distributes it.
The famine devastates Palestine as well, and Jacob twice sends his sons to buy wheat from Egypt. Joseph recognises them but doesn't let them know who he is. Several times he tests them to make them realise the wrong they have done and to see if they are really sorry. He finally reveals that he is their brother. There's a mixture of joy, fears and forgiveness. Pharoah invites Jacob and all his family to come and live in Egypt. Their descendants will stay there for several centuries up until Moses.
The bible´gives us the key to the saga of Joseph: God has brought good out of something bad.

... Then his brothers themselves came and bowed down before him. *"Here we are before you as your slaves,"* they said. But Joseph said to them: *"Don't be afraid; I can't put myself in the place of God. You plotted evil against me, but God turned it into good, in order to preserve the lives of many people who are alive today because of what happened."*

Dream

Dreams have always fascinated people. Where do dreams come from ? The Bible often shows God using dreams to speak to men and women.

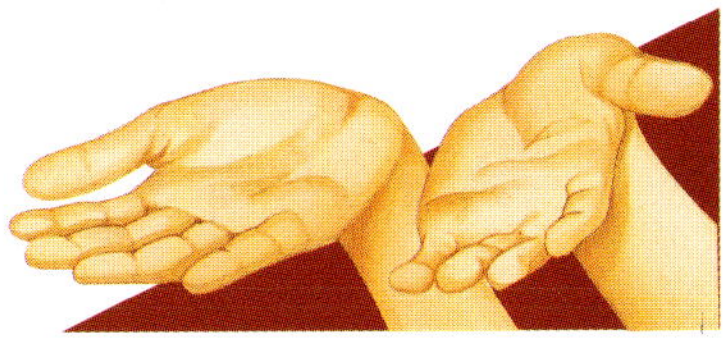

Famine

In olden days this disaster struck often. In Palestine it was the result of shortage of rain or parasites. In Egypt it was usually due to the irregular level of the River Nile.

Today

Dignity

Jealousy

Why are people jealous ? It's as if other people's success hurts them, or other people's beauty is unbearable. It's as if other people's talents make our gifts seem weak. Jealousy is a really serious evil. A jealous person never wants anyone else to be great or praised or happy.

Ill will

As a result of jealousy and envy, people end up wanting to do wrong. It becomes important to look for sly and roundabout ways to ruin other people's happiness, their reputation or even their life.

Selling

Sometimes people do "sell" their own brother, sister or neighbour. This happens whenever they do them harm, say hateful things about them or mock them. It's the same when they act violently, or threaten them, tell lies about them or ruin their reputation. Selling is deadly !

Dreaming

Everyone has dreamt of being great or working wonders. Everyone has dreamt of making the world a better place with new inventions or discoveries. God has given the gift of dreaming to everyone, but dreaming is not enough. You have to roll your sleeves up to make your dreams work !

Happiness

Having no food or work is horrible, but there's another famine, more horrible than lack of food. It's a famine that takes its toll on many people. It's when people are stripped of dignity and respect, deprived of love and starved of happiness. It's when people lack the warm and friendly presence of other people.

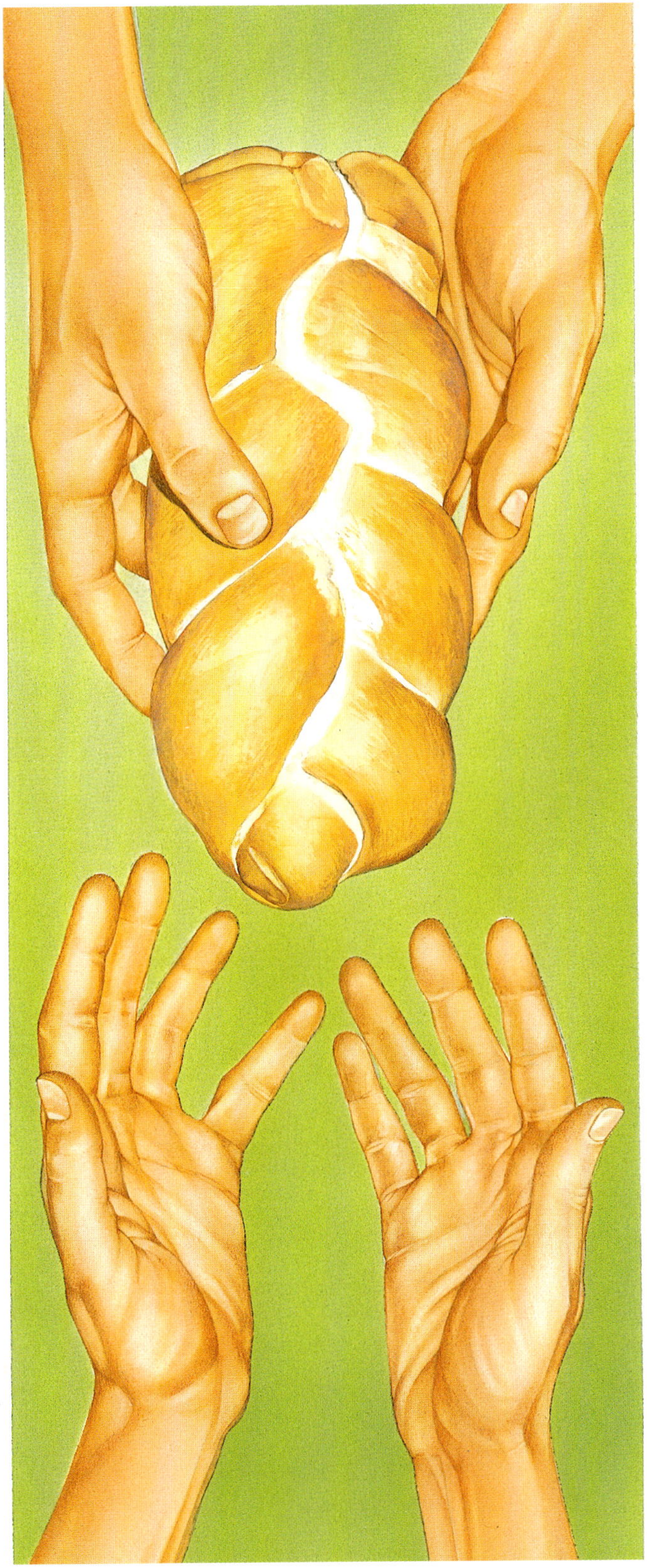

God is different

Wicked people
can sell their neighbours
by mocking them
and laughing behind their backs.
God is different.
God never laughs at anyone.
and always rushes to the defence
of the children of the earth.

Wicked people
can sharpen their tongues
attacking their neighbours
and tearing them apart
with their jealous claws.
God is different
God never wounds anyone.
but is always pleased
when the children of the earth
are successful and joyful.

God does not want one single child
of the earth
to be short of a comforting hand.
God gives everyone,
every day,
a tender and nourishing love.
It's called our daily bread !

Your family

Most people know their brothers and sisters, parents, grandparents, uncles, aunts, and cousins. You can get to know the names of your great-grandparents and other members of your family.

Your family tree

Start with all the people you already know, and you will be able to make your family tree.

Generally you put the following signs on the tree:

For men use the symbol: ♂

For women use the symbol: ♀

To begin, make a note of those you already know and then build it up piece by piece.

Here's an example of Nicholas's family tree:

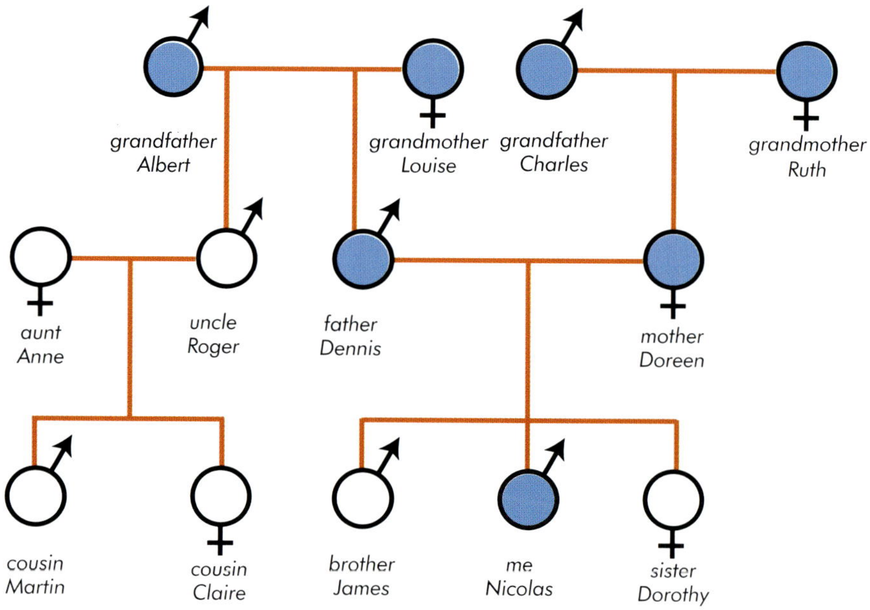

You're not alone

You might like to write down the dates of birth of your family, and to find out which area or country they came from. You'll find your roots and discover that you're part of a family and that each family is part of the great human family.

Abraham's family

In Abraham's time, nearly 4000 years ago, no one had any identity cards or family records. You knew who you were by recalling the names of your ancestors. So Joseph could call himself: "Joseph, son of Jacob, son of Isaac, son of Abraham".

Joseph's family history

You've heard the story of Joseph and his ancestors in this book. You now know how to make his family tree:

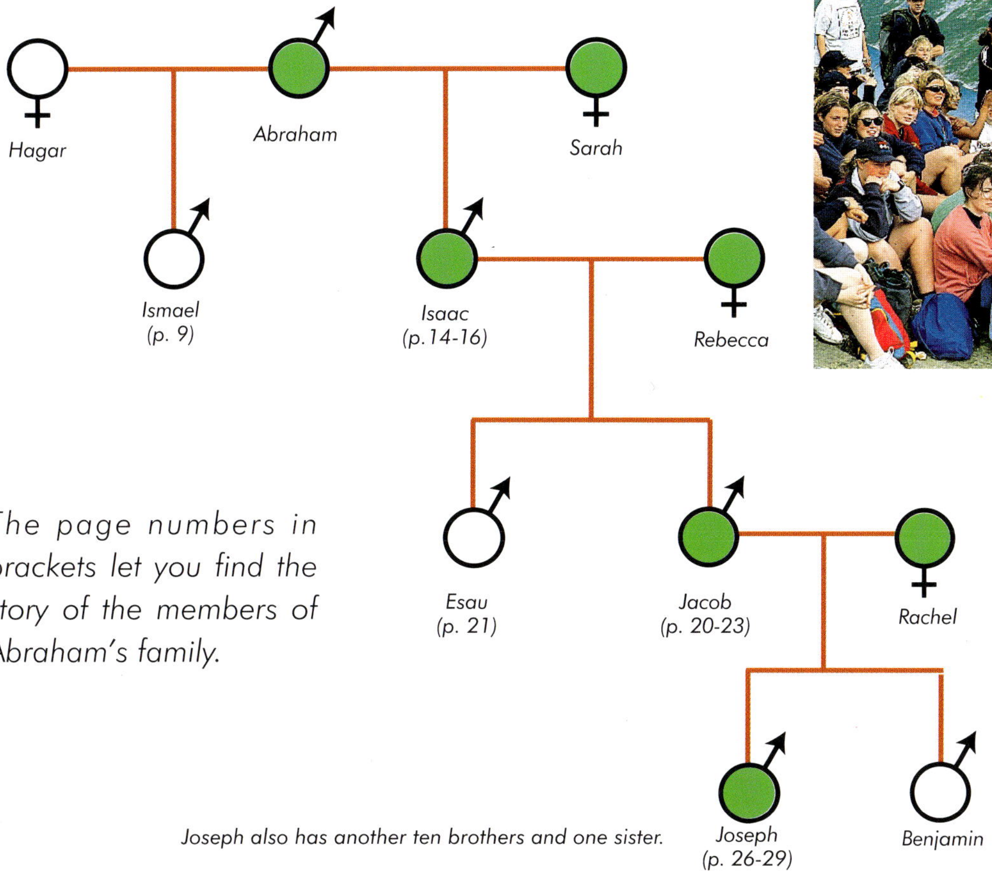

Joseph also has another ten brothers and one sister.

The page numbers in brackets let you find the story of the members of Abraham's family.

All families

God chose Abraham and his family.
Through Abraham God has chosen "all the families of the earth": no one is left out of the great human family, and no one is excluded from God's love.

The Junior Bible

The Junior Bible series brings you books to enjoy.

You will hear the story of God's love
at work from the very beginning and still at work today.

Through stories, poetry, history and prayers.
you will learn about the love of God
in the lives of men and women through all the ups and downs
of their journey as the People of God.

God is still gathering a people today –
the Church is this pilgrim people who share a journey
of prayer
of celebration
of faith
of love and service
especially of people in need.

The migrations of Abraham's family along the Fertile Crescent

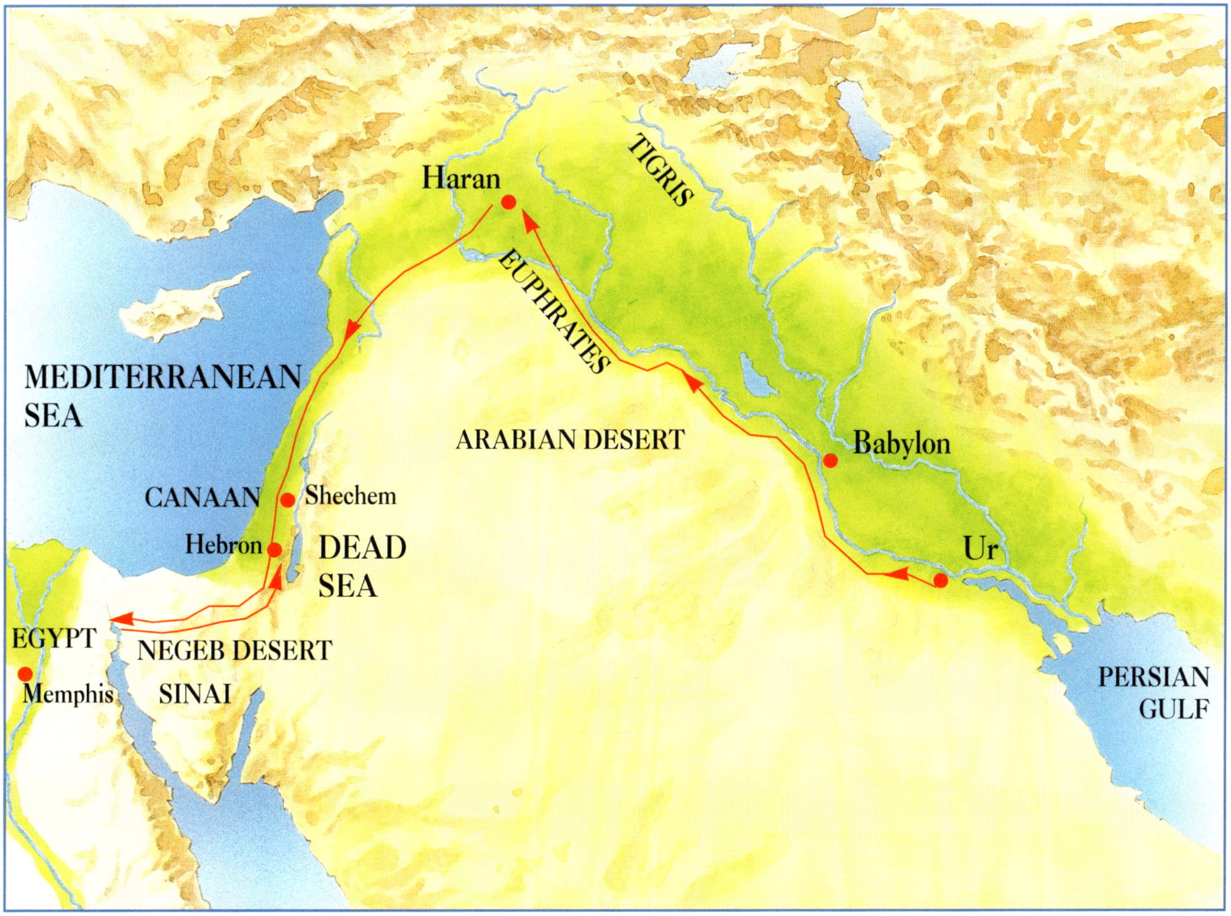

TEXTS

Liam KELLY - Anne WHITE

Albert HARI - Charles SINGER

PICTURE RESEARCH

Sandrine WINTER

PHOTOGRAPHY

Frantisek ZVARDON

Gabriel LOISON

Patrice THÉBAULT

ILLUSTRATORS

Mariano VALSESIA

Betti FERRERO

MIA. Milan Illustrations Agency

LAYOUT

Studio Graphique B.BAYLE

Nihil obstat: George Stokes. censor
Imprimatur: Rt Rev Arthur Barrow VG
Brentwood 23 June 1998

MATTHEW JAMES PUBLISHING LTD
19 WELLINGTON CLOSE

CHELMSFORD, ESSEX CM1 2EE

ISBN 1 898366 47 0

Printed in Italy by Albagraf, Pomezia